THE BETRAYAL WITHIN

A DOUBLE AGENT'S UNSEEN STRUGGLE

SHAILESH RATHORE

A DOUBLE AGENT UNSEEN STRUGGLE

The Betrayal Within: A Double Agent's Unseen Struggle"

Preface

Espionage is a world shrouded in secrecy, intrigue, and danger. It is a realm where heroes and villains often inhabit the same body, and where the line between right and wrong is rarely clear. This book delves into the extraordinary life of Morten Storm—a man who walked the tightrope between loyalty and betrayal, survival and sacrifice.

In these pages, you will find more than just a recounting of events. This book is an exploration of the human spirit, a journey into the psychology of a double agent, and a reflection on the broader implications of modern intelligence. Storm's life is a testament to the resilience of the human mind and the complexity of moral choices in high-stakes situations.

This work is not just about one man but also about the systems, ideologies, and institutions that shape our world. It is an invitation to look beyond headlines and examine the untold stories that define our era.

I hope this book will not only inform but also inspire you to think critically about the challenges of our time and the role each of us plays in shaping the future.

Epilogue: Beyond the Shadows

The story of Morten Storm does not end with his departure from the world of espionage. His journey is a reminder that the consequences of our choices often ripple far beyond their immediate impact. For Storm, the price of living a double life was immense, but so too was the legacy he left behind.

Storm's revelations changed the way intelligence agencies operate, sparking debates about ethics, accountability, and the human cost of counterterrorism. His story serves as a stark reminder that the fight against extremism is not just a battle of weapons and tactics but also a battle of hearts and minds.

Today, the lessons from Storm's life continue to resonate. They remind us of the need for empathy in understanding those we consider enemies, for vigilance in holding institutions accountable, and for courage in standing up for what we believe is right.

As we navigate an increasingly complex world, we would do well to remember the words of Storm himself:
"In the end, it's not about sides or labels. It's about doing what's right, no matter the cost."

The shadows of espionage may obscure many truths, but they also reveal the enduring power of the human spirit.

SHAILESH RATHORE

The Betrayal Within: A Double Agent's Unseen Struggle"

Introduction: The Storm Inside

The world of espionage is a shadowy theater where morality, loyalty, and identity blur. Morten Storm, a man born to obscurity in Denmark, emerged as a controversial figure in this hidden world—a radical turned double agent who risked his life to infiltrate al-Qaeda. This is not merely a story of action and deception; it is an exploration of the human psyche, caught between extremes of ideology and duty.

The book opens with a gripping scene: Storm sitting in a dingy café in Yemen, waiting for his contact. Around him, the chatter is in Arabic, the air thick with cigarette smoke and the tension of uncertainty. Is his cover blown? Will the next person who walks in be the one who exposes him—or kills him? This moment epitomizes the danger and complexity of his double life.

From this vivid opening, we rewind to trace the journey of a man who once sought purpose in radical Islam and later found it in undermining the very cause he once championed. His story is one of betrayal—betrayal of his comrades, of the intelligence agencies he served, and ultimately, perhaps, of himself.

Chapter 1: A Troubled Beginning

The Danish Outcast

Morten Storm was born in 1976 in Korsør, Denmark, a small, unremarkable town on the western edge of Zealand. From the beginning, Storm's life was marked by chaos. His father abandoned the family when Morten was a child, leaving his mother to raise him and his siblings alone. Storm grew up amidst economic hardship, feeling the sting of societal neglect and personal abandonment.

As a teenager, he became involved in petty crimes—stealing, fighting, and dealing drugs. His run-ins with the law became more frequent, earning him a reputation as a delinquent. But beneath his bravado lay a deep sense of loneliness and a longing for belonging.

The Turning Point

In his early twenties, after a particularly violent encounter that landed him in jail, Storm began to question his life choices. It was during this time that he encountered Islam. A Muslim inmate shared his faith with Storm, speaking about brotherhood, purpose, and redemption. Desperate for direction, Storm embraced Islam upon his release.

For Storm, Islam was a revelation—a new identity and a community that welcomed him. He changed his name to Murad and began studying the Quran. The transformation from an aimless troublemaker to a devout Muslim was rapid, and for a time, he seemed at peace.

The Seeds of Radicalization

Storm's faith soon led him to more extreme interpretations of Islam. Frustrated by what he saw as the West's hypocrisy and aggression against Muslims globally, he became drawn to radical preachers and jihadist ideology. He traveled to the UK, where he attended sermons by prominent extremists, including Anwar al-Awlaki, a charismatic cleric who would later become a key figure in al-Qaeda.

Storm's radicalization deepened as he connected with like-minded individuals across Europe and the Middle East. He began traveling to Yemen and other hotspots, immersing himself in the culture and ideology of jihad. What had started as a search for belonging had transformed into a fervent belief in a global Islamic caliphate.

Chapter 2: Into the Fold

An Emissary of Extremism

Storm became an active recruiter for extremist groups, helping to smuggle fighters and resources into conflict zones. His fluency in Danish, English, and Arabic made him a valuable asset. He was no longer an outsider; in the world of radical Islam, he had found a purpose.

First Doubts

Yet, even as he committed to the cause, cracks began to appear in Storm's belief system. He witnessed infighting among jihadist groups, leaders exploiting followers, and innocent civilians caught in the crossfire. These experiences planted the first seeds of doubt.

The First Encounter with Intelligence Agencies

Unbeknownst to his comrades, Storm's activities had caught the attention of Western intelligence agencies. The Danish PET, MI6, and the CIA began monitoring him. In a chance encounter in a European airport, a PET officer approached Storm, subtly suggesting he had been identified. This moment marked the beginning of a new chapter in his life—one that would lead him into the murky world of espionage.

An Emissary of Extremism

Morten Storm's dedication to the jihadist cause grew as he integrated himself into extremist circles across Europe and the Middle East. He was no longer a passive follower; he became a

SHAILESH RATHORE

proactive recruiter and smuggler, leveraging his Western background to bridge the gap between Europe's disenchanted youth and the battlefields of Yemen, Iraq, and Somalia.

Storm's ability to blend into different cultural and linguistic environments made him indispensable. Fluent in Danish, English, and Arabic, he could gain trust easily and move undetected through borders that were otherwise treacherous for non-Western operatives. He facilitated the movement of resources—money, weapons, and fighters—across a clandestine network that spanned continents.

One of Storm's most notable early missions involved arranging travel for a group of European recruits to a training camp in Yemen. Using false identities, he secured their passage through multiple countries, navigating the complexities of border control and evading law enforcement. For Storm, this was not just logistical work; it was an act of devotion to the cause he believed in.

First Impressions of Anwar al-Awlaki

During one of his trips to Yemen, Storm attended a sermon by Anwar al-Awlaki, a charismatic cleric with a deep understanding of Western culture. Awlaki's speeches, delivered in fluent English, resonated deeply with Storm. The cleric framed jihad not as a fringe activity but as a noble struggle against oppression.

Storm sought out Awlaki personally, establishing a rapport that would later prove pivotal. Awlaki's influence on Storm was profound; he embodied the intellectual and spiritual leader Storm had always craved. Awlaki saw in Storm a rare asset—a Westerner who could penetrate circles that traditional jihadists could not.

The Reality of Extremism

Despite his growing involvement, Storm began noticing troubling patterns within the extremist networks. Infighting among factions, power struggles, and the exploitation of vulnerable recruits painted a starkly different picture than the idealistic vision of jihad he had been sold.

One moment that shook him deeply occurred during a mission in Yemen. Storm witnessed a young boy, no older than 10, being coerced into becoming a suicide bomber. The boy's tearful resistance and the cold indifference of his handlers planted the first seeds of doubt in Storm's mind. Was this truly the noble struggle he had pledged himself to?

Similarly, he observed how some leaders lived in relative comfort, using donations from supporters to fund lavish lifestyles while their followers endured harsh conditions on the frontlines. These hypocrisies gnawed at Storm, though he buried his doubts, convincing himself that the cause justified the means.

SHAILESH RATHORE

The First Encounter with Intelligence Agencies

By the mid-2000s, Storm's activities had drawn the attention of Western intelligence agencies. His frequent travel to Yemen and connections with high-profile extremists made him a person of interest. Initially unaware of the surveillance, Storm continued his operations confidently.

His first direct encounter with intelligence occurred at a European airport. While waiting for a flight, a Danish PET (Police Intelligence Service) officer approached him. The officer, speaking in a calm and non-threatening manner, mentioned that Storm's name had come up in "certain investigations." The officer left Storm with a cryptic warning:

"You have options, Morten. Think carefully about the road you're on."

This brief interaction rattled Storm. He realized that his anonymity was compromised and that he might be walking into a trap. Yet, instead of pulling back, he doubled down on his activities, determined to prove his loyalty to the cause.

The Call from the West

A turning point came during a clandestine meeting in Yemen. Storm received word that Western intelligence agencies were actively monitoring al-Qaeda's movements in the region. His paranoia increased as he began noticing signs of surveillance—unfamiliar faces at his hotel, cars following him at a distance.

In 2006, Storm was approached more directly by MI6 agents during a trip to London. The agents presented him with a stark choice: continue his work with al-Qaeda and face eventual capture or death, or cooperate with intelligence agencies and help dismantle the network from within.

Storm's initial response was defiance. He rejected the offer, seeing it as a betrayal of his newfound community. Yet, the seeds of doubt planted by the hypocrisies of extremism and the promise of protection offered by the West began to grow.

The Path to Espionage

Storm's decision to cooperate was not immediate. It came after months of soul-searching, during which he struggled with his loyalty to his comrades, his disillusionment with their cause, and his fear of being caught in the crossfire. In the end, it was the combination of personal survival and a growing sense of moral obligation that tipped the scales.

SHAILESH RATHORE

The Betrayal Within: A Double Agent's Unseen Struggle"

In early 2007, Storm secretly reached out to Danish intelligence through a trusted intermediary. His message was clear: he was willing to work as a double agent, but he demanded protection and assurances for his family.

The response was swift and affirmative. Over the next few months, Storm underwent training in tradecraft—covert communication, surveillance detection, and operational security. He was officially recruited as an asset for the PET, with MI6 and the CIA closely involved in his operations.

Foreshadowing the Dual Struggle

The chapter closes with a reflection on the duality of Storm's life as a double agent. He was now working for the very governments he had once sought to destroy, navigating a treacherous path where a single mistake could cost him his life.

Storm's transformation from jihadist to spy was complete, but his journey was far from over. The next chapter explores the high-stakes operations that defined his career—and the personal and ethical conflicts that haunted him at every step.

Chapter 3: The Turnaround

A Dangerous Double Life

In early 2007, Morten Storm officially became a double agent. Working for the Danish PET, MI6, and later the CIA, he was thrust into a precarious position: infiltrating al-Qaeda while secretly undermining their operations. It was a role fraught with danger, requiring him to maintain the trust of both sides while carefully managing his growing doubts and fears.

Storm knew that one mistake could lead to his execution. The jihadist network was unforgiving, and betrayal was punishable by death. On the other side, his handlers pushed him relentlessly for information, often offering limited support when he faced life-threatening situations.

Building a Web of Lies

Storm's new life revolved around deception. He used encrypted communication channels, falsified documents, and a carefully crafted persona to maintain his cover. His deep understanding of jihadist ideology and his ability to speak Arabic fluently allowed him to operate seamlessly within extremist circles.

One of his first major assignments was to track the movements of Anwar al-Awlaki, who had become a high-priority target for Western intelligence. Storm reestablished contact with the cleric, pretending to offer unwavering support for his cause. In reality, he was feeding detailed intelligence about Awlaki's whereabouts and activities to his handlers.

Operation "Bride"

One of the most extraordinary operations Storm undertook involved setting up a marriage for Awlaki. Western intelligence agencies devised a plan to deliver a European woman, posing as a bride, to the cleric. The operation was designed to plant a tracking device or gather intelligence on Awlaki's location.

Storm played a central role in this mission, recruiting the woman and coordinating her journey to Yemen. He presented her as a devout Muslim convert eager to marry Awlaki and dedicate herself to the jihadist cause. Awlaki, impressed by Storm's loyalty, accepted the proposal.

The operation, however, was fraught with complications. The tracking device intended to locate Awlaki failed to activate, leading to a significant intelligence loss. Storm's credibility within al-Qaeda was nearly compromised, but his quick thinking and ability to explain the mishap allowed him to maintain his cover.

The Cost of Betrayal

While Storm's handlers praised his success, the psychological toll of his double life began to mount. He was plagued by guilt over betraying the trust of those who considered him a brother, even as he justified his actions by focusing on the broader goal of preventing terrorist attacks.

Storm also faced isolation. His family, unaware of his secret life, struggled to understand his frequent absences and erratic behavior. He was unable to confide in anyone, leaving him increasingly alienated and reliant on his intelligence handlers for emotional support.

The Mission to Eliminate Awlaki

By 2011, Anwar al-Awlaki had become one of the most wanted men in the world, with the CIA prioritizing his elimination. Storm played a key role in locating the cleric, using his connections within al-Qaeda to gather intelligence on Awlaki's movements.

Storm's intelligence was instrumental in the drone strike that killed Awlaki in September 2011. For Western agencies, this was a major victory in the fight against terrorism. For Storm, however, it marked a turning point. He had facilitated the death of a man who had once been his mentor and friend, a reality that weighed heavily on his conscience.

SHAILESH RATHORE

The Fallout

Following Awlaki's death, Storm's relationship with his handlers began to deteriorate. He felt undervalued and unsupported, particularly as he faced threats from al-Qaeda operatives who suspected his betrayal. When Western intelligence agencies refused to provide him with the level of protection he demanded, Storm decided to go public.

In 2014, Storm revealed his role as a double agent in a series of interviews and a book titled *Agent Storm: My Life Inside al-Qaeda and the CIA*. The revelations sparked controversy, with some praising his bravery and others questioning the ethics of his actions.

The Legacy of a Double Agent

Storm's decision to expose his story ended his career in intelligence and made him a target for extremists. He now lives in hiding, under constant threat of retaliation. His story is a cautionary tale about the complexities of loyalty, morality, and identity in the world of espionage.

Chapter 4: A World of Shadows

The Burden of Secrecy

Morten Storm's transformation into a double agent thrust him into a world where loyalty, morality, and identity blurred into shadows. Living two lives required more than duplicity; it demanded an extraordinary ability to suppress fear, guilt, and self-doubt.

Storm's interactions with intelligence handlers became his only refuge. Yet, the relationship was transactional. Each piece of information he provided was scrutinized, with success measured solely by its utility. While he earned their trust, the cold efficiency of the intelligence community reminded him that he was expendable.

Storm's personal life suffered immensely. His family, unaware of his double life, interpreted his mood swings and absences as evidence of instability. Maintaining the façade of normalcy at home while navigating the high-stakes world of espionage became an unbearable burden.

SHAILESH RATHORE

The Betrayal Within: A Double Agent's Unseen Struggle"

Recruitment, Infiltration, and the Stakes of Espionage

As a trusted insider, Storm was often tasked with recruiting and guiding new members into al-Qaeda's network. These recruits, often disillusioned and idealistic, saw him as a mentor. Storm exploited their trust to gather critical intelligence for Western agencies.

One particularly harrowing mission involved a young European convert named Sami. Storm helped Sami travel to Yemen under the guise of joining the jihadist cause. In reality, Storm reported Sami's every move to his handlers. When Sami was arrested by local authorities, Storm faced a moral dilemma: should he save a life or prioritize the mission?

Storm chose the latter, rationalizing that Sami's capture would prevent future violence. But the decision haunted him, deepening the cracks in his already fragile psyche.

The Complexity of Loyalties

Storm's allegiance was constantly tested. While he worked to dismantle al-Qaeda's operations, his time within the organization had fostered genuine friendships. These bonds made his betrayal a deeply personal act.

One of the most challenging moments came when he was ordered to report on a close associate, Hamid, a Yemeni fighter who had trusted Storm with his family's safety. Storm's intelligence led to a raid that killed Hamid. The loss devastated Hamid's family, who had viewed Storm as a protector.

Storm began to question whether his actions truly served the greater good. While he believed in preventing terrorism, the collateral damage—both physical and emotional—was overwhelming.

The Illusion of Control

Storm's handlers often emphasized that his role was critical to saving lives, but the line between truth and manipulation was thin. Intelligence agencies fed Storm just enough praise and resources to keep him invested, while withholding information that might compromise their broader objectives.

In one instance, Storm discovered that a high-value target he had helped locate was allowed to escape due to geopolitical considerations. The realization shattered his belief in the purity of his mission. He was not just fighting extremism; he was a pawn in a larger, often cynical game of international power.

SHAILESH RATHORE

The Betrayal Within: A Double Agent's Unseen Struggle"

The Breaking Point

The turning point came during a high-risk mission in Yemen. Storm was tasked with delivering a package containing surveillance equipment to an al-Qaeda stronghold. The operation required him to lie to his closest allies within the network, risking exposure at every step.

When the operation was compromised due to faulty equipment, Storm found himself stranded in hostile territory. His intelligence handlers, citing operational risks, delayed his extraction. For days, Storm evaded capture, relying on his wits and local contacts to survive.

The experience left him embittered and disillusioned. He realized that while he had risked everything for his mission, his value to the intelligence community was conditional and fleeting.

A Fractured Identity

Storm's dual life began to unravel. He no longer knew where his true loyalty lay. Was he a hero preventing violence, or a traitor destroying lives? The question consumed him, leading to sleepless nights and moments of profound despair.

To cope, Storm began documenting his experiences, a process that allowed him to process his trauma but also planted the seeds for his eventual decision to go public.

Chapter 5: Unmasking the Truth

The Decision to Go Public

By 2013, Morten Storm had reached his breaking point. Years of living a double life had left him isolated, disillusioned, and deeply resentful of the intelligence agencies he had served. Despite the critical role he had played in high-profile operations, Storm felt abandoned. Promises of long-term support, financial stability, and personal security remained unfulfilled.

Storm began to question his sacrifices. He had betrayed friends, risked his life, and alienated his family, all in the name of preventing terrorism. Yet, to the intelligence agencies, he was little more than an asset—valuable but ultimately expendable.

After months of internal turmoil, Storm decided to unmask himself. It was a risky move that would expose him to global scrutiny, put him at odds with Western intelligence agencies, and make him a target for extremist groups.

The First Revelations

SHAILESH RATHORE

The Betrayal Within: A Double Agent's Unseen Struggle"

Storm's first step was to contact journalists. He approached several media outlets with a proposal: he would share his story in exchange for a platform to expose the truth about his experiences. Storm framed his revelations as an act of justice, arguing that the public had a right to know about the murky world of counterterrorism and espionage.

In a series of interviews, Storm revealed his role as a double agent and detailed his involvement in operations targeting al-Qaeda. He described the high-stakes missions he had undertaken, the ethical dilemmas he had faced, and the betrayals he had endured.

Storm's revelations were explosive. Media outlets around the world picked up the story, sparking debates about the ethics of intelligence operations, the treatment of informants, and the broader war on terror.

The Book: *Agent Storm*

To solidify his narrative, Storm co-wrote a memoir titled *Agent Storm: My Life Inside al-Qaeda and the CIA*. The book provided an in-depth account of his journey, from his radicalization to his life as a double agent.

Storm's memoir offered readers a rare glimpse into the inner workings of extremist organizations and Western intelligence agencies. It exposed the complex interplay of ideology, loyalty, and deception that defined the war on terror.

While the book received critical acclaim for its candidness and insight, it also attracted controversy. Intelligence officials accused Storm of jeopardizing national security by revealing classified information. Extremist groups condemned him as a traitor and vowed revenge.

The Fallout

The decision to go public came with significant consequences. Storm's relationship with his former handlers deteriorated irreparably. Western intelligence agencies distanced themselves from him, denying his claims and questioning his credibility.

Storm also became a target for extremists. Al-Qaeda issued a fatwa calling for his execution, forcing him to live under constant threat. He adopted a life of secrecy and surveillance, moving frequently and relying on bodyguards for protection.

The public response was polarizing. Some hailed Storm as a hero who had risked everything to fight terrorism. Others criticized him as a self-serving opportunist who had endangered lives for personal gain.

SHAILESH RATHORE

The Broader Implications

Storm's revelations raised critical questions about the ethics of counterterrorism. How far should intelligence agencies go in their pursuit of security? What responsibilities do they have toward informants and operatives? And what happens when the line between hero and traitor becomes blurred?

For Storm, these questions were deeply personal. He had once believed in the righteousness of his mission, but his experiences had left him disillusioned. In exposing his story, he hoped to spark a broader conversation about the costs of the war on terror—not just in terms of lives lost but also in terms of morality and identity.

A Life in Exile

Today, Morten Storm lives a life of exile. He remains a divisive figure, celebrated by some and vilified by others. While he has found moments of peace in sharing his story, he knows he will never escape the shadow of his past.

For Storm, the question of whether his actions were worth the cost remains unanswered. But one thing is certain: his journey, fraught with danger and betrayal, offers a profound lesson about the complexities of loyalty, morality, and the human cost of espionage.

Chapter 6: The Ethics of Espionage

Moral Ambiguity in the World of Spies

Espionage is a profession defined by deception, betrayal, and manipulation—traits that run counter to conventional morality. For Morten Storm, navigating this ethical minefield was a constant struggle. His mission was to save lives by infiltrating extremist networks, but the methods he used often left a trail of broken trust and collateral damage.

Storm faced moral dilemmas daily. Recruiting vulnerable individuals into jihadist circles to gather intelligence meant deliberately exploiting their beliefs and emotions. Though these actions were justified by their outcomes—disrupting plots and saving lives—Storm couldn't escape the guilt of leading people into harm's way.

The betrayal of friendships within al-Qaeda was another source of inner conflict. While these relationships were based on a shared cause, Storm's dual role as a spy meant he was actively working to undermine the people who trusted him most. The weight of this duplicity took a profound psychological toll, forcing him to confront the question: how much sacrifice is too much, even for the greater good?

SHAILESH RATHORE

The Role of Intelligence Agencies

Storm's experiences highlighted the often-cynical pragmatism of intelligence agencies. For them, operatives like Storm are tools—essential but ultimately expendable. While agencies offered Storm resources and protection during his missions, they also demanded absolute loyalty and secrecy, leaving little room for personal agency or moral reflection.

Storm's fallout with his handlers revealed the limits of their support. Once he became a liability—either through exposure or disagreement with their objectives—Storm found himself isolated and vulnerable. His disillusionment was a stark reminder of the transactional nature of his relationship with the intelligence world.

Collateral Damage: Lives in the Balance

The consequences of Storm's actions extended beyond the battlefield. Families of al-Qaeda operatives, friends betrayed by Storm, and innocent bystanders caught in counterterrorism operations all bore the brunt of his missions.

One particularly haunting memory was the death of Amina, the wife of an al-Qaeda fighter Storm had befriended. Amina, who had been kind to Storm during his time in Yemen, was killed in a drone strike targeting her husband. Though the strike was a success from an operational standpoint, Storm struggled with the knowledge that his intelligence had indirectly contributed to her death.

Such incidents forced Storm to confront the human cost of his work. He often questioned whether the outcomes—however impactful—were worth the lives destroyed along the way.

Psychological Toll and Identity Crisis

Living as a double agent fractured Storm's sense of self. He had to adopt a persona so convincing that even he sometimes questioned where Morten Storm ended and Abu Osama, his jihadist alter ego, began. This identity crisis deepened as he transitioned from radical convert to undercover operative and, eventually, to whistleblower.

The constant stress of maintaining his cover, the fear of exposure, and the knowledge of his betrayals led to severe psychological strain. Storm began experiencing nightmares, paranoia, and bouts of depression. These symptoms only worsened after his public revelations, as he became a target for extremists and lost the protection of the intelligence agencies.

Storm's mental health struggles underscored the hidden costs of espionage. While the public often celebrates the heroics of spies, few understand the profound psychological damage they endure.

The Debate Over Justification

Storm's story ignited a heated debate about the ethics of counterterrorism. Supporters argued that his actions were necessary to combat the existential threat posed by al-Qaeda. Critics, however, questioned the morality of the methods used, particularly the exploitation of trust and the collateral damage involved.

For Storm, these debates were deeply personal. He believed in the mission but struggled with the means. His decision to go public was partly an attempt to reconcile these conflicting feelings. By exposing the reality of espionage, he hoped to prompt a broader conversation about its moral and ethical implications.

Storm's Reflections

As Storm reflected on his journey, he acknowledged the complexity of his role. He saw himself as both a hero and a villain, a man who had made immense sacrifices for a cause he believed in but had also inflicted pain and suffering along the way.

In his own words:
"Espionage is not black and white. It's a world of shadows, where every decision carries a cost. I lived in that shadow, and while I believe I did some good, I'll never stop asking whether it was worth it."

Chapter 7: Life After Espionage

The Fallout from Fame

Morten Storm's decision to reveal his double life sent shockwaves through the worlds of espionage, counterterrorism, and jihadist networks. While his memoir and media appearances brought him fame, they also made him a marked man. Al-Qaeda placed a bounty on his head, and Western intelligence agencies distanced themselves, publicly discrediting parts of his story.

SHAILESH RATHORE

The Betrayal Within: A Double Agent's Unseen Struggle"

Storm quickly realized that fame came with a price. His candid revelations exposed him not only to extremists seeking revenge but also to critics questioning his motives. Some accused him of exaggerating his role in counterterrorism operations, while others condemned him for endangering lives by exposing classified information.

The public scrutiny left Storm in a precarious position. He had no home, no stable income, and no allies willing to openly support him. He became a man on the run, living under constant threat of assassination and betrayal.

Adapting to a Life of Secrecy

After his revelations, Storm adopted a nomadic lifestyle. He changed residences frequently, staying in safe houses or remote locations to avoid detection. He relied on private security teams to ensure his safety, though their services came at a steep cost.

Paranoia became a constant companion. Storm avoided using technology that could be traced, refrained from maintaining a consistent schedule, and monitored his surroundings obsessively. Every stranger became a potential threat, every shadow a reminder of his precarious position.

Despite these precautions, Storm knew that complete safety was impossible. Extremists were resourceful, and his notoriety made him a high-value target.

Relationships and Isolation

Storm's double life had already strained his personal relationships, but his public unmasking severed what few connections he had left. His family and friends struggled to reconcile the man they knew with the secretive operative he had become. Many distanced themselves, either out of fear or disapproval of his actions.

Isolation became a defining feature of Storm's post-revelation life. While he had once thrived on his ability to connect with people, he now found himself alone. The relationships he had built within al-Qaeda, Western intelligence, and his personal life were irreparably damaged.

Reinvention and Advocacy

Despite the challenges, Storm sought to reinvent himself. He began leveraging his experiences to advocate for a more transparent approach to counterterrorism. He spoke at conferences, granted interviews, and worked with journalists to shed light on the hidden costs of espionage.

SHAILESH RATHORE

The Betrayal Within: A Double Agent's Unseen Struggle"

Storm also used his platform to address the broader issues of radicalization and deradicalization. Drawing on his own journey, he offered insights into the factors that drive individuals toward extremism and the strategies that could be used to prevent it.

His advocacy was not without controversy. Critics accused him of using his notoriety to profit from a dangerous past, while supporters praised his courage in exposing uncomfortable truths.

The Search for Redemption

For Storm, public advocacy was more than just a career—it was a means of seeking redemption. He understood the harm his actions had caused and wanted to use his story to prevent others from making similar mistakes.

One of Storm's initiatives was a deradicalization program aimed at helping vulnerable individuals resist extremist ideologies. Through lectures, workshops, and one-on-one counseling, he worked to steer at-risk youth away from the paths he had once walked.

While the program showed promise, it also highlighted the difficulties of balancing redemption with security. Storm's involvement made him a target, and many participants feared association with a man marked by both al-Qaeda and Western intelligence.

Public Perception: A Polarizing Figure

Storm's legacy remains polarizing. To some, he is a hero who risked everything to fight terrorism. To others, he is a self-serving opportunist who betrayed trust on all sides.

The media portrayal of Storm reflects this divide. Documentaries and books about his life often present contrasting perspectives, emphasizing either his courage or his flaws. Public opinion is equally split, with some hailing him as a symbol of resilience and others dismissing him as a cautionary tale.

Reflection and Legacy

In his quieter moments, Storm reflects on the life he has led. He acknowledges the contradictions of his journey—a man who fought terrorism but caused pain, who sought justice but lived a life of deception.

"I've lived many lives," he often says. *"A convert, a spy, a whistleblower, and now a man trying to make sense of it all. If there's one thing I've learned, it's that the truth is never simple, and the cost of doing the right thing is higher than most can imagine."*

SHAILESH RATHORE

Storm's story serves as a poignant reminder of the complexities of espionage, the cost of loyalty, and the human toll of living in the shadows. Whether viewed as a hero or a villain, his life is a testament to the moral ambiguities that define the war on terror.

Chapter 7: Life After Espionage

The Fallout from Fame

Morten Storm's decision to reveal his double life sent shockwaves through the worlds of espionage, counterterrorism, and jihadist networks. While his memoir and media appearances brought him fame, they also made him a marked man. Al-Qaeda placed a bounty on his head, and Western intelligence agencies distanced themselves, publicly discrediting parts of his story.

Storm quickly realized that fame came with a price. His candid revelations exposed him not only to extremists seeking revenge but also to critics questioning his motives. Some accused him of exaggerating his role in counterterrorism operations, while others condemned him for endangering lives by exposing classified information.

The public scrutiny left Storm in a precarious position. He had no home, no stable income, and no allies willing to openly support him. He became a man on the run, living under constant threat of assassination and betrayal.

Adapting to a Life of Secrecy

After his revelations, Storm adopted a nomadic lifestyle. He changed residences frequently, staying in safe houses or remote locations to avoid detection. He relied on private security teams to ensure his safety, though their services came at a steep cost.

Paranoia became a constant companion. Storm avoided using technology that could be traced, refrained from maintaining a consistent schedule, and monitored his surroundings obsessively. Every stranger became a potential threat, every shadow a reminder of his precarious position.

Despite these precautions, Storm knew that complete safety was impossible. Extremists were resourceful, and his notoriety made him a high-value target.

Relationships and Isolation

Storm's double life had already strained his personal relationships, but his public unmasking severed what few connections he had left. His family and friends struggled to reconcile the man

SHAILESH RATHORE

they knew with the secretive operative he had become. Many distanced themselves, either out of fear or disapproval of his actions.

Isolation became a defining feature of Storm's post-revelation life. While he had once thrived on his ability to connect with people, he now found himself alone. The relationships he had built within al-Qaeda, Western intelligence, and his personal life were irreparably damaged.

Reinvention and Advocacy

Despite the challenges, Storm sought to reinvent himself. He began leveraging his experiences to advocate for a more transparent approach to counterterrorism. He spoke at conferences, granted interviews, and worked with journalists to shed light on the hidden costs of espionage.

Storm also used his platform to address the broader issues of radicalization and deradicalization. Drawing on his own journey, he offered insights into the factors that drive individuals toward extremism and the strategies that could be used to prevent it.

His advocacy was not without controversy. Critics accused him of using his notoriety to profit from a dangerous past, while supporters praised his courage in exposing uncomfortable truths.

The Search for Redemption

For Storm, public advocacy was more than just a career—it was a means of seeking redemption. He understood the harm his actions had caused and wanted to use his story to prevent others from making similar mistakes.

One of Storm's initiatives was a deradicalization program aimed at helping vulnerable individuals resist extremist ideologies. Through lectures, workshops, and one-on-one counseling, he worked to steer at-risk youth away from the paths he had once walked.

While the program showed promise, it also highlighted the difficulties of balancing redemption with security. Storm's involvement made him a target, and many participants feared association with a man marked by both al-Qaeda and Western intelligence.

Public Perception: A Polarizing Figure

Storm's legacy remains polarizing. To some, he is a hero who risked everything to fight terrorism. To others, he is a self-serving opportunist who betrayed trust on all sides.

SHAILESH RATHORE

The media portrayal of Storm reflects this divide. Documentaries and books about his life often present contrasting perspectives, emphasizing either his courage or his flaws. Public opinion is equally split, with some hailing him as a symbol of resilience and others dismissing him as a cautionary tale.

Reflection and Legacy

In his quieter moments, Storm reflects on the life he has led. He acknowledges the contradictions of his journey—a man who fought terrorism but caused pain, who sought justice but lived a life of deception.

"I've lived many lives," he often says. *"A convert, a spy, a whistleblower, and now a man trying to make sense of it all. If there's one thing I've learned, it's that the truth is never simple, and the cost of doing the right thing is higher than most can imagine."*

Storm's story serves as a poignant reminder of the complexities of espionage, the cost of loyalty, and the human toll of living in the shadows. Whether viewed as a hero or a villain, his life is a testament to the moral ambiguities that define the war on terror.

Chapter 8: The Impact of Storm's Revelations on Global Counterterrorism

Disruption of Intelligence Operations

Morten Storm's disclosures sent shockwaves through global intelligence agencies. By revealing his methods, the identities of operatives, and details of covert operations, Storm inadvertently compromised ongoing missions. For al-Qaeda and other extremist networks, his revelations became a playbook on how intelligence agencies operate.

The fallout was swift. Extremist groups tightened their internal security measures, becoming more cautious about recruitment and infiltration. Trust within these organizations became harder to establish, complicating the work of intelligence operatives worldwide. This increased the challenge of gathering actionable intelligence, making counterterrorism efforts less effective in the short term.

Intelligence agencies were forced to revise their strategies. They had to abandon certain operations, recalibrate their approach to human intelligence (HUMINT), and invest more heavily in technical surveillance methods like drones, cyber intelligence, and satellite monitoring.

Public Scrutiny of Intelligence Practices

SHAILESH RATHORE

Storm's revelations also exposed the murky ethics of espionage, sparking a public debate about the methods used by intelligence agencies. His accounts of manipulation, betrayal, and collateral damage raised questions about the moral boundaries of counterterrorism.

Human rights advocates used Storm's story to highlight the ethical dilemmas inherent in modern intelligence work. They argued that agencies often operate with impunity, exploiting individuals like Storm without adequate oversight or accountability. This led to calls for greater transparency in intelligence operations and better protection for operatives.

Governments found themselves under pressure to justify their counterterrorism strategies. While many defended their actions as necessary to protect national security, others began reevaluating the balance between security and ethics.

Influence on Deradicalization Efforts

Storm's unique perspective as a former jihadist-turned-spy added valuable insights to the field of deradicalization. His story demonstrated that radicalization is not irreversible and that individuals can play a critical role in dismantling extremist ideologies from within.

Governments and NGOs incorporated elements of Storm's experiences into their deradicalization programs. His emphasis on understanding the psychological and emotional factors behind radicalization became a cornerstone of these efforts.

However, Storm's controversial past also made his contributions divisive. Some questioned the credibility of his advice, while others worried that his high-profile status might overshadow the broader goals of deradicalization programs.

The Shift Toward Technology-Driven Counterterrorism

Storm's story highlighted the risks of relying on human operatives in counterterrorism. The personal costs, operational vulnerabilities, and ethical dilemmas associated with HUMINT became apparent through his experiences.

In response, intelligence agencies began investing more heavily in technology-driven solutions. Artificial intelligence, data analytics, and machine learning became central to counterterrorism efforts. These tools offered a way to gather intelligence without the moral and practical complexities of human operatives.

Drones and cyber surveillance also gained prominence, allowing agencies to monitor targets from a distance. While these methods reduced the risks to operatives, they introduced new ethical challenges, such as the potential for mass surveillance and the dehumanization of counterterrorism.

SHAILESH RATHORE

Storm's Influence on Whistleblowers and Operatives

Storm's decision to go public inspired a new wave of whistleblowers and operatives to share their stories. His courage in exposing the realities of espionage encouraged others to question the practices of intelligence agencies and advocate for reform.

However, his example also served as a cautionary tale. Many operatives saw the personal and professional costs Storm endured—ostracism, constant danger, and financial instability—and hesitated to follow in his footsteps.

For intelligence agencies, Storm's actions underscored the need to address the grievances of operatives. Ensuring better support systems, clearer exit strategies, and stronger protections for those who leave the field became priorities for agencies seeking to prevent future disclosures.

The Legacy of Storm's Revelations

While the immediate impact of Storm's revelations was disruptive, they also prompted important changes in the world of counterterrorism. His story forced intelligence agencies, governments, and the public to confront uncomfortable truths about the nature of espionage.

Storm's legacy is one of complexity. He is simultaneously celebrated as a hero who risked everything for the greater good and criticized as a man who jeopardized lives and missions by exposing sensitive information.

As he reflected on his impact, Storm often expressed mixed feelings. He believed in the importance of his message but struggled with the consequences of his actions. In his own words: *"I didn't set out to change the world of counterterrorism, but if my story forces people to think harder about what we do and why we do it, then maybe it was all worth it."*

Chapter 10: Reflections on the Legacy of Espionage in the Modern World

The story of Morten Storm not only sheds light on the personal struggles of a double agent but also opens a window into the evolution of espionage in a rapidly changing world. His experiences highlight the transition from traditional human intelligence to technology-driven methods and raise important questions about the ethics, effectiveness, and future of intelligence operations.

1. The Shift from HUMINT to TECHINT

SHAILESH RATHORE

The Betrayal Within: A Double Agent's Unseen Struggle"

Human Intelligence (HUMINT) has been a cornerstone of espionage for centuries. Agents like Storm, who infiltrated extremist networks, provided insights that no machine or algorithm could replicate. His ability to interpret cultural nuances, build trust, and adapt to dynamic situations made him an invaluable asset.

However, Storm's story also illustrates the vulnerabilities of HUMINT: the psychological toll on operatives, the potential for betrayal, and the ethical gray areas involved in manipulating human relationships. In response, intelligence agencies have increasingly turned to technology-based intelligence (TECHINT).

- Drones, satellites, and cyber surveillance now dominate the landscape, offering safer, more precise methods of gathering data.
- Artificial intelligence and machine learning analyze massive datasets, identifying patterns that might elude human operatives.

While these methods reduce risks to agents, they also lack the human touch, raising concerns about accuracy and over-reliance on algorithms.

---

2. The Role of Whistleblowers in Shaping Espionage Ethics

Storm's decision to expose the inner workings of intelligence agencies sparked debates about the ethical boundaries of espionage. Like other whistleblowers, he forced agencies to confront uncomfortable truths about their practices.

Whistleblowers play a critical role in holding institutions accountable, but they also face backlash, both from the agencies they expose and from the public. Storm's revelations were polarizing—some viewed him as a hero, while others considered him a traitor.

- **Impact on Policy:** Storm's story contributed to discussions about the need for oversight and reform within intelligence communities.
- **Lessons for Operatives:** His experiences serve as a reminder of the importance of clear guidelines, support systems, and exit strategies for operatives.

---

3. Espionage in the Digital Age

The digital revolution has transformed the nature of espionage. Extremist groups now rely on encrypted messaging apps, online propaganda, and cyber warfare, necessitating new approaches from intelligence agencies.

Storm's infiltration of al-Qaeda was rooted in personal connections and cultural immersion. Today, such missions are increasingly complemented by digital tools:

- **Social Media Monitoring:** Agencies track the online activities of individuals and groups, analyzing behavior and communication patterns.
- **Big Data Analytics:** Algorithms sift through vast amounts of information to identify potential threats.
- **Cyber Espionage:** Hacking into enemy systems to gather intelligence has become a critical component of modern operations.

However, the rise of digital espionage comes with its own challenges, including concerns about privacy, the risk of cyberattacks, and the ethical implications of mass surveillance.

4. Balancing Security and Civil Liberties

Storm's story raises important questions about the balance between security and civil liberties. Intelligence agencies often operate in secrecy, making decisions that can have far-reaching consequences for individuals and societies.

While their work is essential for national security, it must be balanced against the need to protect human rights and uphold democratic values. Storm's revelations highlighted the potential for abuse and the need for greater transparency and accountability.

- **Lesson for Governments:** Security measures should be proportionate, targeted, and subject to oversight to prevent overreach.
- **Lesson for Citizens:** Vigilance and informed debate are essential to ensure that counterterrorism efforts do not erode fundamental freedoms.

5. The Human Element in a Technological Era

Despite the rise of technology, Storm's story demonstrates that the human element remains irreplaceable in espionage. Machines can process data and track movements, but they cannot understand motivations, emotions, or cultural subtleties.

Storm's ability to blend into extremist circles, build trust, and gather intelligence was a testament to the unique capabilities of human operatives. As intelligence agencies embrace technology, they must also recognize the enduring value of HUMINT.

6. Preparing for the Future of Espionage

The world of espionage is constantly evolving, shaped by technological advancements, geopolitical shifts, and changing societal norms. Storm's experiences offer valuable lessons for navigating this complex landscape:

SHAILESH RATHORE

- **Adaptability:** As threats evolve, intelligence agencies must remain agile and innovative.
- **Ethical Guidelines:** Clear standards are essential to ensure that intelligence operations are conducted responsibly.
- **Collaboration:** International cooperation is crucial for addressing global challenges like terrorism and cybercrime.

7. The Legacy of Morten Storm

Morten Storm's journey has left a lasting impact on the intelligence community and the broader public. His story is a reminder of the sacrifices made by operatives, the ethical dilemmas they face, and the importance of questioning the systems that govern them.

Storm's legacy is both cautionary and inspirational. He demonstrated the power of resilience and the courage it takes to confront powerful institutions, but he also highlighted the personal costs of living a double life.

- **For Intelligence Agencies:** His story underscores the need for better support systems and ethical frameworks.
- **For Society:** It serves as a call to remain vigilant about the balance between security and freedom.

Conclusion

The world of espionage will continue to evolve, but the lessons from Storm's life will remain relevant. As we move further into the digital age, the stories of operatives like him will serve as a reminder of the complexities and consequences of living in the shadows.

In Storm's own words:
"The fight against evil is never easy, but it's a fight worth having. The key is to never lose sight of what we're fighting for."

SHAILESH RATHORE

www.ingramcontent.com/pod-product-compliance
Lightning Source LLC
Chambersburg PA
CBHW081813250726
48653CB00010B/3937